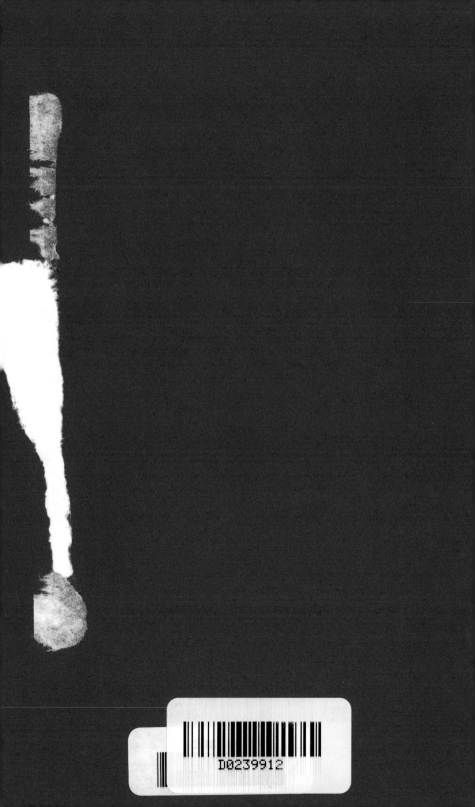

the
Perfect Family

The Aga Man

*The Aga is Mrs New-Kitchen's lifestyle statement
to her girlfriends*

the Perfect Family

SOCIAL STEREOTYPES FROM THE
Telegraph magazine

Victoria Mather
and
Sue Macartney-Snape

JOHN MURRAY

For
Margaret Gardner
In memory of Alexander Walker
V.M.

and

For
Tiko
S.M.-S.

———————————————

Text © 2003 and 2004 Daily Telegraph plc
and Victoria Mather

Illustrations © 2003 and 2004 Daily Telegraph plc
and Sue Macartney-Snape

First published in Great Britain in 2004 by John Murray (Publishers)
A division of Hodder Headline

The right of Victoria Mather and Sue Macartney-Snape to be identified
as the Authors of the Work has been asserted by them in accordance with the
Copyright, Designs and Patents Act 1988.

1 3 5 7 9 10 8 6 4 2

A CIP catalogue record for this title is available from the British Library

ISBN 0 7195 6697 5

Typeset in Monotype Bembo 11.5/15pt by
Palimpsest Book Production Limited, Polmont, Stirlingshire

Printed and bound in Spain by Bookprint S.L., Barcelona

Hodder Headline policy is to use papers that are natural, renewable and recyclable
products and made from wood grown in sustainable forests. The logging and
manufacturing processes are expected to conform to the environmental
regulations of the country of origin.

John Murray (Publishers)
338 Euston Road
London NW1 3BH

Foreword

INFURIATING THOUGH IT may be for Victoria Mather and Sue Macartney-Snape to be told by callow, youngish journalists, 'Of course I was offered Social Stereotypes first: but I turned it down', they can afford to laugh, secure in the knowledge that the original idea and its name was theirs, and that they proposed it to Emma Soames for the Saturday *Telegraph Magazine*.

Accordingly they smile superior smiles and ponder skewering the pretenders in three hundred words and a brilliant illustration – 'The Deluded Journalist' perhaps. The single definite article before a threatened subject creates a promise of social satirical satisfaction for the reader as potent as H. M. Bateman's 'The man who . . .'

Bateman, Osbert Lancaster, 'Spy' and Ronald Searle have all been cited as ancestors of Sue Macartney-Snape's drawings. The wit of Saki, Evelyn Waugh, Nancy Mitford and Dorothy Parker has been compared to Victoria Mather's stiletto prose. Mitford seems to me to be the nearest parallel, but I can imagine Victoria installed in the 1930s Algonquin and responding imperiously to Frank Case's knock on the door, 'Is there a gentleman in your room?' with, 'Wait a minute, I'll ask him.'

I imagine their collaboration to be rather like a songwriting method: lyricist provides title; composer incorporates it strategically in the most memorable phrase of a foot-tapping tune; lyric writer sorts the rest of the lyric to sit happily on the composer's notes. A similar give and take must go on with our devilish duo. However, this is not to imply that Victoria has all the ideas: the inspiration is shared fairly equally. Victoria reports that she gets calls from the Antipodes, where Sue now spends a lot of her time, with suggestions. And sometimes they seem to think with a single mind: not long ago Victoria had an idea, just then the telephone rang and

5

a voice several thousand miles away enquired, 'Do you think we should do "The Disorganised Woman"?'

'The Perfect Family' exuberantly includes in one Macartney-Snape drawing/one Mather paragraph no fewer than five stereotypes who could all justify an individual column – with a dog thrown in, along with an off-sketch trendy society photographer.

There's reckless generosity for you, characteristic of the collaborators. When Craig Charles, a colleague of Victoria's and mine, was imprisoned in South London (later acquitted), Victoria called to say, 'Do you think we should "spring" him?' I would like to see Sue's vision of Victoria manhandling Craig over the walls of Brixton prison: but the point of the gals' book is that they deal wittily and magisterially not with specific people but with sagely selected stereotypes.

Sue Macartney-Snape may never have contemplated arranging a prison escape but her generosity is shown in the prodigal wealth and precision of detail which she lavishes on her drawings – the defining shoes, the generously low-flying bosoms, the plummeting stomachs, the scrawny limbs, the exact accessories.

Down Under Sue may have relished realising 'The Awful [Australian] Boyfriend', egged on by Victoria's cutting prose: 'Granny says beadily that perhaps the knife and fork are new to Australia.' The family's solution is to ship their daughter to Italy where she discovers Italian waiters. Now they 'suddenly have fond memories of Dean, who at least spoke a version of English'.

There are two old colloquial clichés that sum up this brilliant pair. Sue Macartney-Snape's observation suggests she has 'eyes on stalks'; to Victoria Mather I can only say, 'Back in the knife box, Miss Sharp.'

Ned Sherrin
Spring 2004

Acknowledgements

Social Stereotypes has gone global. This year *The Party Blonde*, *The Embarrassing Parents* and *The Appalling Guests* were published in Australia. It seems extraordinary to Sue and me that ten years after the first stereotype – The Working Mother – was published we are, like the hoofers in Sondheim's *Follies*, still here, and celebrating on the other side of the world. The party at Christie's, Melbourne, wouldn't have been possible without expert masterminding by Barbara Higgins, a mercy dash to the bottle shop by Jane Guy, cocktail strategy by Ned Guy and flowers by my Australian family, John, Gwen, Gary, Sharon, Teagan and Mitchell Mather.

Stereotypes has always had a generous support system. The merriment of the series, and of my life, is consistently enhanced by Nicholas Coleridge and Nicky Haslam. Many of the characters herein are written and drawn from inspiration by Christopher Fildes, Sue and Douglas Gordon, Annabel Fairfax, Alex and Lizzie Catto, Ann Sadler, Daisy Finer, and Sarah, India and Tilly Standing, adjudicators of cool. The Andreae/Chetwode stereotypes thinktank continues in Toulouse; Sarah Long is Sue's muse, and A.A. Gill is entirely to blame for The Airport Check-In. Ned Sherrin has been wrongly accused of being my father, yet nothing could be more paternalistic than his friendship. How else would I be able to catch up on *The Archers*? At the *Telegraph* we're particularly indebted to Denis Piggott, Jeremy Farr, and wonderful Sandie Elsden and Juliet Caulfield. At John Murray we thank Roland Philipps, Caroline Knox and Caroline Westmore for her unfailing courtesy.

Victoria Mather
Hampshire, 2004

Was it really such a good idea to have a family photograph?

The Perfect Family

IAN IS ON the mobile, Nancy is on the vodka. Was it really such a good idea to have a family photograph to commemorate their wedding anniversary? Gemma's spots are luminous, Jake hasn't washed his hair since he returned from teaching orphans in Peru, and Flossie is having a tantrum entirely justifiable in one forced into bunches and pink frills. Even the charm of society snapper Hugo Burnand has failed to elicit the desired portrayal of familial perfection to be displayed on the piano for years to come. Digital manipulation will be insufficient to conceal Gemma's weight problem; Nancy, inversely thin, is poignantly brittle with desperation. It was, after all, her idea. 'And a damned silly one,' Ian told her at breakfast. 'Gemma might just as well be wearing a burqa – haven't you got a decent dress, girl? And get your hair off your face. Jake looks like a drug addict, and probably is for all we know, since he only ever speaks in grunts, and why is Flossie the only little moppet who disembowels rather than plays with her dolls? I imagine it's too much to hope that she's going to grow up to be a heart surgeon.' When Hugo arrived he was told that the whole damned charade mustn't take too long. 'In the time it takes you to fiddle with your tripod, young man, entire financial markets could have collapsed. I need to be on that telephone.'

Even the dog is embarrassed, regarding Flossie's imitation of Violet Elizabeth Bott with the perplexity of one who never saw the point of the afterthought, born when the marriage was shaky due to Ian's affair with his secretary. When the ordeal is finally over, Nancy offers everyone champagne and chatters too brightly. 'We must have 400 prints for our Christmas card, mustn't we, darling?' The words 'over', 'dead' and 'body' rattle out of Ian's study like gunfire. Sometimes there's nothing quite as sad as family groups.

The Disorganised Woman

HARRIET KNOWS SHE'S put the car keys somewhere, she must have done, because she came back from Waitrose in the car after the emergency mercy dash for soap powder. But as she staggered in with the dog biscuits and a six-pack of loo paper – why does it run out so quickly? – the heel of her shoe snapped. She finally found glue in the sewing basket, and was then distracted by the crossword in a month-old newspaper: challenging, as she couldn't find her glasses because they were on her head, so just as she got round to doing the washing, Lucy brought the children back from school. Goodness, can it be that time already? And Marcus has to be taken to his extra Japanese class. Harriet drops armfuls of greying knickers, and Lucy, always so pearly and flossed, says 'Honestly, Harriet, I can take Marcus. Alice has to go to extra quantum physics, and it's in the same direction. Why don't I give both the children tea?'

Despite tea happening every day, it always takes Harriet by surprise. She's bought some organic sausages but, like the car keys, they've vanished to the Lost Planet. Or a Safe Place, along with Harriet's passport and diamond earrings. Oh, joy – the keys are under the fine for failing to pay the congestion charge. Harriet meant to, but then her mobile rang (frantic scrabbling in her handbag) because Marcus had got concussion during football practice in Battersea Park. Now the fine's up to £140. Once, when she did pay Ken's frightful little tax at the machine in Thresher's in Dover Street, Harriet got a parking ticket because her car was on a yellow line. Honestly, it was only two minutes, and she was on her way to a charity meeting about Aids orphans in Africa. Friends cherish the story of how, on her wedding day, Harriet didn't have time to wash her hair.

*Harriet's car keys have vanished to a Safe Place,
along with her passport and diamond earrings*

Life's tough when you've done everything

The Bored Playboy

GUIDO IS BOTH disgruntled and dyspeptic. He had too much to drink at Mark's Club at lunch – the 'too much' of three glasses of burgundy would not have been enough in his heyday and then he lost at blackjack at the Clermont. Really, what else was there to do? He'd already bought a picture at Christie's in the morning. He only came to London from Buenos Aires via New York for Annabel Goldsmith's book launch at the Ritz, and has stayed on because there seemed so little point in going to St Moritz. Dreadful people nowadays, some of them even made their own money. Since Botox, the women all look like freeze-dried little marmots, nervous faces popping up from their fur collars. Guido used to have a sportsman's room at the Palace, basically a cupboard in which to hang his clothes. The bed was inconsequential since he always slept in other people's. Now he should go to St Tropez. But can he bear the ennui of eating the crudités in Club 55 again and seeing Sir Donald Gosling brought ashore from his boat that looks like an NCP car park?

Style, that is what has gone from Guido's world. Onassis, Niarchos (Guido liked his Greeks), Jimmy Goldsmith – all gone. Only Nicky Haslam is reliably amusing these days. If Nicky goes to the Monaco Grand Prix in distressed black-leather cargo pants and a singlet, it might be worth accepting Rainier's invitation. Guido is amused by so little now, this could just bring a smile to lips otherwise only pleasurably exercised by a cigar. Ascot? Better just to go and have lunch in White's tent. The Riviera? Terrible traffic jams. Capri? Ghastly trippers. Once Guido played polo; now, if there's a helicopter, he'll heave himself to the Veuve Clicquot Gold Cup. Life's tough when you've done everything.

The Airport Check-In

MARTHA VON WEEVIL is absolutely incensed. She has had to wait at least 15 seconds in the first class queue – she's checked on her Rolex – because the wretched woman behind the desk is having problems with her computer. 'Do you know who my husband is? Adrian, show her your Premier card. It's really so simple, you don't need your machine, he always has seat 2A. And could you telephone ahead to the captain and make sure the temperature is adjusted to 21 degrees. The trouble with British Airways is that your planes are too hot.' Martha's adjacency to the crowd jostling for Economy is making her querulous. Only a rope is separating her from the Sharon and Darren tendency, en route to Florida, no doubt, with their squalling children. People who actually check in luggage because they haven't got their own homes to stay in. Martha and Adrian don't do luggage. It is a very long time since Martha has travelled with anything except her tranquillisers. Of course, if they go and stay with friends, or it's Simon Murray's board meeting in Phuket, then they FedEx their luggage ahead. The jollity of the huddled masses next door to her, lumpen with guitars, cameras and music systems, none of which will fit in the overhead lockers, appals Martha. They actually seem to be looking forward to the journey. Later, her skeletal figure is dwarfed by the BA flatbed, while Shirley, Megan and Terry, having wedged themselves into the world traveller seats, are downing the Bailey's Irish Cream and playing with the seat-back tellies. Martha drinks nothing but flat water and never touches her personal screen in case she chips her nail varnish. She flicks at *Vanity Fair*, then dons an eyeshade. Taking his walk to avoid DVT, Adrian notices that there are quite smart people at the back of the bus weathering the trip by reading *Berlin*.

*Martha's adjacency to the merry masses jostling for Economy
is making her querulous*

*A sunny, lazy peace descends on guns replete
with Pomerol, picnic and Lady Braggart's sloe vodka*

The Shooting Party

LADY BRAGGART PRIDES herself on the picnics at Glen Porridge. Not for her the floury bap, soggy with tomato and plastic ham. Others may rejoice in the romance of their 'piece' eaten on the heathery hill, but Sonia Braggart hasn't employed two nice girls from Lucy Morton's just to stuff buns with packet filth. At midday the Land Rover, driven by MacTavish the gardener, leaves the lodge laden with quiches warm from the Aga, chicken legs rolled in oatmeal and homemade scotch eggs. The fruitcake is dark and wet with treacle and brandy. There are both flapjacks and chocolate brownies. Bump, bump, up on to the moor to Spittal of Tester, the Braggarts' favoured luncheon spot during the grouse season, and the nice girls lay out tartan rugs and cool the beers in the burn. Sir Hector's buttery white burgundy is in a chill bag, his Pomerol in the picnic basket, improbably alongside two bottles of Avon's Oh-So-Soft lotion. It's the new secret weapon against the midge, according to Murdo in the gun shop in Abersturdy. Archie Tweedbutt gave it a trial run on the Twelfth, walking up at Blair Thistle, and pronounces success between mouthfuls of Taleggio focaccia.

A sunny, lazy peace descends on guns replete with Pomerol, picnic and Lady Braggart's sloe vodka. 'Slow death, more like,' says Rory Strathplaid, lolling back for a siesta in the heather, one sleepy eye on the absurdly pretty girl from London in a silly hat. She's asking Archie, in clipped St Mary's Calne, about the hazards of midges up the kilt. 'Ticks are trickier, m'dear, especially when you have to burn them off with a cigar.' Sir Hector has just offered his best Havanas around liberally. The nice girls brought the newspapers for those keen on a quick look at the *FT* before ferreting for their mobiles in their sporrans. The bees are buzzing, the grouse are flying well, all is right with this little world.

The Dotty Driver

CLODAGH IS A marvellous guide to Woldshire. 'Now, Desmond, the Cunninghams live just here on the left, splendid Palladian house' – screech of brakes – 'I'll reverse so you can see the gargoyles at the gates, Grinling Gibbons they think, cast in limestone. Now what on earth is that stupid little man on a tractor doing behind me?' She serenely accelerates, leaving a melange of hay bales strewn across the road. 'Now you'll love the farmers' market, I always park in the undertakers, luckily no one else seems to think of it.' This is probably because access to Messrs Black & Black reads No Entry, but prohibitive road signs have never held any fear for Clodagh. 'They don't apply to one, darling.' Nor does she ever lock the car – 'So common' – leaving the Westie in the back seat, asleep on the dry cleaning. Loading Desmond with organic honey and Woldshire lamb, Clodagh threatens to take him the scenic route to lunch. 'Now, I have to take you through Pettifer St Mary, Charles II hid in the marvellous oak tree on the green. Now is it right or left? I always get confused. Lanes, lanes, lanes, the country's a nightmare, isn't it?'

Desmond, clinging to his seatbelt, has the distinct feeling that he's with a rural Mrs Stitch. Any moment, and the BMW will be rattling through the gardens of assorted peasantry, a leafy variation of that *Scoop* progress along the pavements of Piccadilly. The indicator is an anomaly to Clodagh, and when declaring that she absolutely knows The Vyne House is to the right, she swings confidently to the left trilling, 'I just say watch or bracelet to myself and it all seems to work. You'll love the Bo-Vynes, they do ripping Bloody Marys.' On the journey home, Clodagh sings Cole Porter, adheres magisterially to the centre side of the road and when timidly admonished says, 'What, darling? Am I driving? I thought you were.'

*Desmond, clinging to his seatbelt, has the distinct feeling
that he's with a rural Mrs Stitch*

Jake is a jet-propelled accident

The Toddler

JAKE HAS JUST become ambulatory. He has gone from being a gurgling, dormant heap kicking his little heels in Granny's Silver Cross pram ('No grandson of mine is going to have one of those three-wheeler pushchair things. The vulgarity!'), to being a jet-propelled accident. Tania has been to casualty so many times she's terrified they're going to put Jake on the at-risk register. The Wandsworth house which had seemed such a marvellous buy – in the 'Toast Rack', knocked-through to a point where it's miraculous it has an inside wall to stand on – is now fraught with peril. The wooden floors might be a poem in *House & Garden*, for Jake they are a skating rink and he hasn't yet mastered a stop mechanism. Tania has spent hours in Mothercare buying protective covers for all the plugs so Jake can't stick his fingers into the mains. The kitchen cupboards have had to be fitted with little safety catches so Jake can't swig the bleach. (Neither Tania nor the Australian nanny can now get into the cupboards either, so an alcohol shortage looms.)

The stairs are Jake's favourite activity zone, so Tania has had to teach him how to go down them backwards, by painstaking demonstration. A year ago she was running her own company, now she is crawling crab-wise down her own staircase, bottom-first. And her back is killing her because of all the time bent double like a hairpin holding Jake's little hand. Granny has said the magic word 'Reins!' and headed off to The White House for a pair in blue leather, despite Tania's delicate fears about the naffness of reins, regardless of their desirability. 'Mummy, reins haven't yet made a comeback like the dummy.' The word dummy had such an emetic effect on the grandmotherly sensibilities that a scene was only averted by Jake finally grasping the cat's tail, eliciting squeals on both sides, followed by the tinkling crash of broken china.

The Hair Colourist

KEVIN SAYS INTO the mirror, 'Who did our colour last, modom?' which makes Angela feel crushed and vulnerable. She's already had her confidence severely shaken by the fact that Hair Fayre, which was so comfortingly old-fashioned and run by Jacqui, has metamorphosed into Topiary. 'We thought it was more cutting-edge,' says Kevin without any evident sense of irony. Angela Popplewell sees no reason for cutting-edge in Alderly Edge, but everyone said she had to go to Kevin – 'Come on, Angie, give yourself a bit of a makeover, love. Do you good after the hysterectomy. Kevin's a babe.'

So now she is being patronised by an androgynous bully who's waving a limp wrist at the shampooist with instructions to mix 'a lot of P389 for this one, dearie'. Kevin then flexes his latex gloves. He is certainly not going to risk dermatitis by applying Juicyblonde's 'Hot Ash' without protection. The smell of bleach is such that Angela vividly remembers stories in the *Daily Mail* of women whose coiffure has turned purple and dropped out in clumps after the ministrations of rogue colourists. Now Kevin has reduced her head to a hedgehog of BacoFoil envelopes and is bunging her under a hot lamp with three editions of *Hello!* featuring people she neither recognises nor wants to. Kevin has Angela completely in his power, for she can hardly run out of Topiary in her black nylon gown, head bristling with foil. He regards her speculatively, head on one side, glasses glinting, reducing Angela to an abject specimen of middle age. Aeons later, looking at her ashy, stripy new self in the mirror, Angela feels as if her hair belongs to someone else. In her embarrassment and haste to leave Topiary for ever, she tips Kevin far too much.

Angela is being patronised by an androgynous bully

Guy and Emma are sitting in Lady Bustard's pew,
where Bustards have sat since Khartoum

The Newcomers
to the Village

LADY BUSTARD IS incensed. The people who've bought Damson
Cottage are sitting in her pew in church. Bustards have been sitting
in that pew since Khartoum, the bones of their ancestors are under
all the most hideous monuments in St Thomas's, and plaques
on the mellow stone walls commemorate their dedication to the
Empire. Indeed, there is a poignant brass memorial to Mungo
Valentine Bustard, who died of snakebite in Kwa Zulu Natal,
right above the pew. You'd think these frightful little down-
from-London people would have known. But Guy and Emma are
oblivious to the tumult raging in Lady Bustard's breast. So far
they have been rather pleased with their social infiltration of
Swallowfield; Emma volunteered to be on the lunch committee
for the clay pigeon shoot and was allowed to make an apple tart.
Guy has become treasurer of the local Conservatives and little
Daisy was asked to read a poem about rabbits at the annual pet
service. They're thrilled they moved to Swallowfield. 'Fulham isn't
what it used to be, the parking's so awful now,' confides Emma
to people who, having crunchy-gravel drives, couldn't care less.
'Now the summer's here, and the builders have left Damson
Cottage, you really must come to a barbecue, we'll have Pimm's.'
Old Swallowfield regards Pimm's as a poor substitute for a proper
drink and barbecues as a suburban abomination.

After the first party everyone says what a pity it is that Emma
wrenched out old Mrs Fothergill's Aga, that Guy and Emma both
seem a bit keen – 'We just had them to bridge, now we're their new
best friends' – and the collective decision is that Emma is pushy. Lady
Bustard declined their invitation on very stiff cream writing paper.

The Grandparents
on Holiday

'NOW, LIBERTY, DON'T do that, or I shall be very, very cross.' When Elizabeth and Douglas decided to take the grandchildren to the Scilly Isles they had no idea they were dealing with a seven-year-old psychotic. Liberty is determined to murder her brother with a fork. Liberty blocked the swimming-pool filter with Rapunzel Barbie's hair. Liberty squirted ketchup on Grandpa's All-Bran. Liberty has broken her shrimping net and says Tresco is so boring, and why doesn't the Island Hotel have a computer room? Each night, lying in bed feeling as if they had been run over, Elizabeth says to Douglas, 'It's all her mother's fault, of course, with her nonsense about laissez-faire parenting.' And Douglas says, 'Well, dear, things are very different to what they were in our day.' They both silently think, as one, of nannies. It was when their son, Roger, divorced in March that they decided to take the grandchildren on a proper bucket-and-spade holiday. Elizabeth envisaged downy heads on the pillow at 7pm, then herself and Douglas bathed and changed for a gracious cocktail in the terrace bar.

On the first night they returned from a mellow dinner with some excellent Shiraz to find Liberty watching repeats of *Sex and the City*. 'Mummy lets me.' Grandma had the television removed, only to have it replaced when the hysterics induced by Liberty's withdrawal symptoms from *EastEnders* caused the family next door – very nice, from Guildford – to complain. Elizabeth's mortification has only been exceeded by young Felix doing wheelies with a dumper truck in his spaghetti hoops, and Liberty telling the waiter that her fish and chips is disgusting yuck.

*Grandma and Grandpa had no idea they were dealing
with infantile psychotics*

*Dean is a hairy-armpitted, eyebrow-bolted, singlet-wearing,
horny-toed sex God*

The Awful Boyfriend

DEAN IS AUSTRALIA'S revenge for all the slacker Etonians who have been sent over to the little antipodean island on a gap year. He is a hairy-armpitted, eyebrow-bolted, singlet-wearing, horny-toed nemesis. Never did the Bracegirdles imagine that their ewe lamb, the divine Candida, would bring home this affront to their sensibilities. Dean comes from Brisbane; the Bracegirdles do not know anyone in Brisbane. Candida met Dean in a pub; the Bracegirdles do not go to pubs. Chuffy Bracegirdle wonders, he really does, why he spent thousands sending Candida to St Mary's when the result of three A-grade A-levels is Dean. Perhaps Dean is a dismal barometer of the total lack of intelligence now required to pass public examinations. Dean drinks beer, Chuffy drinks vintage claret. 'Although he tucks into my Leoville Barton as if it were Kangarouge.' Dean watches sport on television, which means Veronica Bracegirdle feels all six nations have scrummed down in The Mitre House. 'But Chuffy, I wouldn't mind anything as long as he didn't write in his food.' Granny says beadily that perhaps the knife and fork are new to Australia.

Chuffy says he really finds heavy petting in his drawing-room a bit much. 'That bloody gorilla all over Candida, just when I wanted to watch the news. And it upsets the dog.' Candida, doe-eyed with love, is sublimely oblivious to the hackles raised all over her house. Dean is a sex god; she wants to abandon her Italian art course and live with him in a bedsit in Earl's Court while her parents are still muttering about Dean's ignorance of the thank-you letter. Forcefully shipped to Florence, Candida discovers Italian waiters, and the Bracegirdles suddenly have fond memories of Dean, who at least spoke a version of English.

Amelia is illuminated with festive munificence

The Family Christmas

IT WAS AMELIA who thought it would be a lovely idea to have a *really* family Christmas. Her family, of course, not Guy's. 'Darling, we went to your family last year, and don't you think it would be marvellous to be in our own home, with blazing fires, and I can get Terry to come down and design the tree?' Having the new house in Gloucestershire – terribly old, of course, but totally re-done by Terry in taupe – and her adorable IVF twins, Ivo and Holly, who were born at Christmas time, Amelia is illuminated with festive munificence. The Chantry House is lit by a hundred Jo Malone candles, roast geese are in the oven, and the Christmas pudding has been stuffed with £1 coins (boiled, so no germs). So here they all are on Christmas Day, gathered with various degrees of recalcitrance. Amelia's parents, George and Sylvia, are thrilled to be embraced by tropical central heating, life in Rose Cottage being on the lean side of chilly. 'My pension isn't thriving under Mr Brown, Guy, I can tell you. Any tips?' Guy mutters that he's a banker, not a bank manager.

His sister-in-law, Trisha, is a potter married to Steven-with-a-beard. Guy is appalled that he is related to a social worker who lives in Wales. Amelia's trendy brother, Hugo, may be big in IT, but does he have to wear his shirt outside his jeans? As for Trisha and Beardy's children, Jason and the lardy Kirsten who never stops texting (even through Midnight Mass), Guy dreads the twins becoming so unbecoming. Yet he rather fancies Olivia, his unmarried sister-in-law, with her spiky boots and brilliant law degree, a Bridget Jones with a brain. The Christmas spirit cocoons Amelia in her vision of perfection, her parents are delighted not to be doing it themselves, her siblings sneer about Guy, while eating and drinking everything he throws at them out of revenge. All cordially hate each other.

Domestic arrangements are tyrannised by Moat's requirements

The Old Retainer

MOAT HAS BEEN with the Wrottinghams since young Master John, now Sir John, was a baby. Moat has glaucoma, so no one can move any of the furniture in case he trips over an errant armchair while carrying the drinks tray. He is also deaf, so never hears when Lady Wrottingham shrieks for him, and young Wrottinghams have to be sent out to track him through the house by the trail of his dropped cigarette ash. 'Really, John, Moat will have to be retired. I'm quite hoarse with asking him to refill the log basket, and last week he mistook limescale remover for the Goddard's, so the silver looked very peculiar when the High Sheriff came to dinner.' Sir John says he can't imagine Wrotting Hall without Moat. 'He's part of the furniture, old girl.' 'No, he's not, John, he falls over it,' says Lady W crisply. She would also prefer it if Moat didn't help himself from the whisky decanter, then top it up with cold tea. 'John, you'll have to have a word with Moat. I don't mind him drinking whisky – God knows it's the only thing in this house that keeps out the damp – but the tea is very tiresome. I can always tell when he's been at it because of the tea leaves in the decanter.'

But in the unequal struggle of life at Wrotting, domestic arrangements are tyrannised by Moat's requirements. No soup, ever since rheumatism made his shaky action with the ladle at luncheon such a tense experience, although the vicar's wife was most Christian about having Scotch broth poured into the lap of her Jaeger suit. No pheasant, as his gnarled fingers cannot be expected to pluck them any more. No pork: 'The crackling gets stuck in my false teeth, m'lady'. Whenever the despairing Lady W mentions the retirement word, the children say, 'No, Ma, you can't. Moat gives us wicked racing tips.'

The Armchair Spectators

PENNY AND MICHAEL look forward to Wimbledon eagerly every year. They used to go, but it's so much more relaxing to stay at home. Frankly, they missed the action replays. Michael places a whopping order for white burgundy with Corney & Barrow, and they lie back and enjoy the entire fortnight hermetically sealed in the conservatory, blinds down so that no weak ray of sunshine blurs the television screen. Hopes run so high for the Plucky Little Brit that Penny abandons the ironing that she meant to do throughout the afternoon. Michael becomes jitteringly tense; by 5.30 he simply cannot imagine where the second bottle of burgundy went to. 'Bloody Tim Henman, he'll turn us all into alcoholics then go and run a tennis camp on the Costa del Sol.' Penny doesn't know what is harder to forgive: Tim taking them to the edge of every match, the hideous vulgarity of Henmania, or the way in which the silly drip punches the air. She then finds herself doing it when Serena Williams is thrashed in the second set. If there's one thing Penny and Michael are united upon, it is the Williams sisters. It is not because they're black, it is because they wear coloured tennis clothes. Michael can remember Evonne Goolagong – such grace and femininity, not a manufactured muscle machine with bling-bling jewellery. Penny still nurtures a tendresse for John Newcombe, such short shorts. And isn't it funny how McEnroe is now an establishment figure in the commentary box? In his day, with Connors and Borg, the matches were so much more entertaining than the backline sloggers now. Penny and Michael find it very hard to relate to Lleyton Hewitt, a man who wears his base-ball cap the wrong way round. Enveloped in the world of tie-breaks, the only sounds to emerge from the conservatory are exclamations: 'Good shot!' and 'That was definitely out, you stupid man!' Meanwhile, the cat has licked up all the cream for the strawberries.

Penny and Michael's hopes run high for the Plucky Little Brit

The Flag Seller

PHYLLIDA MAY LOOK like somebody's mother up from the country but come National Forget-Me-Not Day in aid of disadvantaged gentry, she is a demon. Phylly and her friends Veronica and Jill have St James's covered. Veronica lurks outside Brooks's, Jill has Christie's and, after they've all had a fortifying breakfast at the Ritz, Phyllida stands outside White's. Her husband, Charlie, is a member, so she raises huge amounts of money by sweetly but firmly embarrassing his friends. 'Come along, Monty, your lunch is going to cost you an extra 20 quid today. You may own half of Woldshire but you never know when Mr Brown is going to disadvantage you, and you may be very glad of Forget-Me-Not sheltered accommodation.' Monty stuffs notes into Phylly's tin and scuttles into the blessed sanctuary of male peace.

Phyllida's post-prandial strategy is to retreat back to the Ritz, standing by the steps to supplicate the likes of Lord Hanson. Jill, meanwhile, moves into pole position to trap Hambros emerging from Wilton's. The Forget-Me-Not Trust did once offer Phyllida the patch outside Peter Jones but she said she didn't see the point in small change. There are no worries about rattling your tin (strictly forbidden by some frightful little law) if you only score folding stuff. By mid-afternoon it's all over. Phyllida, Jill and Veronica go to Fortnum & Mason to stock up on Lapsang Souchong. Then Phyllida meets her daughter, Tweedie, at the Titian, such a nice short exhibition, and takes the bus back to where she's parked her car, thus avoiding the congestion charge. It's been a splendid day, a triumph of modest bullying and flat shoes. Her tin, returned to the charity's meeting point at the GTC, contains £345. 'I say, can we count on you for next year, Mrs Warburton?'

Phyllida stands outside White's, raising huge amounts of money by firmly embarrassing her husband's friends

The Father of the Bride

EVERYONE HAS LEFT for the church, even the bride's mother in a hat that wouldn't fit into the Bentley, and Peregrine is having a lachrymose moment in the hall before Claudia descends the stairs in a cloud of tulle. His little Whizzy. Always such a good baby, smiling and gurgling to order, it seems only months since he popped her on to her first pony. Where's all the time gone? Whizz sailing her Oppi at Bembridge, Whizz singing a solo at the Thomases' carol service. Peregrine remembers his car groaning with luggage and stereoplayer thingies when he took Whizz for her first term at Benenden. And the rows over the ear-piercing, which her mother said was common, and whether she was going to be allowed to go on holiday to Corfu with Simon Scott. 'He's just a friend who's a boy, Pops.' Whizz and her triumph of getting into Oxford. Peregrine has a fortifying sip of brandy at the memory of that telephone call, here in this hall, just the tick of the grandfather clock while everyone held their breath. 'Yes, this is Claudia. Yes? Thank you so very much. That's awfully kind of you.' The dear girl had followed him to his own college.

He was terrified for her golden future all the time she was teaching children in Nepal during her gap year, imagining plague and pestilence. But she's doing marvellously in her job, whatever this PR stuff is. Peregrine only hopes her intended knows what a gem he's getting, although Rupert seems a splendid chap, and one knows his people. And now here she is, glittering in Granny's tiara, his funny bunny. Peregrine harrumphs and says, 'You look lovely, darling, but are you sure? It's not too late to change your mind.' Whizz squeezes his hand and says, 'Let's get in the car.' At the church, as the Trumpet Voluntary swells, she smiles up at him from behind her veil and says, 'Hang on to me, Pops, it's all going to be all right.'

Peregrine is having a lachrymose moment in the hall before
Claudia descends the stairs in a cloud of tulle

Gavin and Amanda have absorbed the wiles of social acceleration:
no past, huge future, the best parties and big houses

The Social Climbers

GAVIN AND AMANDA have napalmed everyone with the news that they are going to dinner with the Effulgents. 'No romantic Valentine's tryst for us,' Amanda has trilled to the school-run mothers at The Snobbery kindergarten. 'But then whoever wants to go out on Valentine's with all those amateur restaurant-goers?' Gavin has stage-whispered to his colleagues at Deutsche Gnome Gromit that he'll be seeing old Eddie Effulgent – implying an intimate gathering – so that any message DGG needs to get over to the proprietor of the *Daily Grind* can be safely confided to him. That the dinner is Lady Effulgent's fundraiser in aid of Dispossessed Pussycats, including 300 guests and an auction of CatArt, has been fabulously glossed over by Gavin and Amanda. They are masters of the charity event as social ladder, the charity committee as social enabler. Amanda is, of course, involved with the Reptilian Gallery, so she mwah-mwahs with the Palumbos, the della Gherardescas, and assorted Oppenheimers. That she can spell none of them is no hindrance to name-dropping, although the words Branston and Forte fall more easily from her lips. Not least because Amanda once worked as a waitress in one of 'dear Rocco's' hotels. She would never tell him that, of course, even if they were ever formally introduced.

As by rodent cunning, Amanda has absorbed the wiles of social acceleration: no past, huge future, the best parties and big houses. Naturally she is too unconfident to wear anything but designer clothes and new jewellery. Now she is baring her whitened teeth at Lady Effulgent and Gavin is clapping Lord Effulgent on the back, 'hoping for a little chat later, my lord'. Out of insecurity, Gavin will bid £10,000 for Damien Hirst's FatCat pickled in Krug.

The Tree Hugger

GIDEON'S PARENTS ARE appalled. After years of expensive education, work experience at Deutsche Gnome and the round-the-world ticket, all they've produced is a hobbit. Of course, at dinner parties Celia says that eco-consciousness is the way forward in the 21st century. 'I mean, look what Prince Charles has achieved with his organic biscuits.' However, Gerald's paternal tolerance is on a knife-edge; only Johnny Walker is standing between him and a carpet-biting rant about the Youth of Today. He expected Gideon to be a master of the universe (in which case it wasn't the cleverest idea to call him Gideon). What he's got is a smelly little toad with a damn silly beard who thinks trees have souls. 'Very iffy pong from his bedroom, Celia. You don't think he's smoking pot, do you? Let me tell you, and the fool Blunkett, that there's zero tolerance in this house.' Celia feels as if intolerance has subsumed her entire life. 'I'm intolerant to wheat, Mum, it's harvested by giant corporations. And you can't have log fires – every time you cut down a tree it screams. Swaths of rainforest are being culled by the forces of capitalism; humanity is going to self-destruct because more paper is needed for the invitations on your mantelpiece.' Only the other day Celia was desperately trying to find where they were supposed to be having drinks with the Whittle-Thompsons, but Gideon had already recycled the card. The newspapers are daily arboreal mass murder.

Fortunately tree-hugging is not an early-morning activity, so Gerald is able to get into his chauffeur-driven car with the *FT* intact. His punishment on his return is a lecture on toxic emissions. 'Only the life-giving oxygen from leaves is between you and death by carbon dioxide, Dad.' All three of them will be infinitely relieved when Gideon goes up to read Planet Regeneration at university.

After years of expensive education,
Gideon has turned out to be a hobbit

The Latimers are so obsequiously grateful to Trudy for babysitting at the last moment that they said, 'Help yourself to anything'

The Babysitter

TRUDY IS DISAPPOINTED by the contents of the Latimers' fridge. 'Usually they have smoked salmon, but all I can find is some old ham,' she says, listlessly poking some delicious jambon cru that Charlotte Latimer was sent by a friend in Seville, who personally knew the pig and had fed it on acorns. The Latimers are so obsequiously grateful to Trudy for babysitting at the last moment that they said, 'Help yourself to anything,' and allowed her to bring pimply Kevin the boyfriend, now slumped in front of Sky Sports. Trudy is so bodily subsumed in her perusal of the fridge that the commentary on its contents emerges in little breathy clouds. 'Fancy some chicken, Kev? Or there's a rocket-and-four-cheese pizza.' Kevin grunts, 'Where are the beers then?'

The gastronomic assessment is interrupted by the shrill wail of a baby whose molars are coming through. Trudy reverses out of the fridge, thunders upstairs and shoves a dummy in his mouth. She then conducts a forensic search of Mrs Latimer's bathroom, trying the Crème de la Mer, and spraying herself with Joy. 'Ugh, bloody horrible.' The baby has now spat out the dummy and is both screaming and rattling the bars of his cot. 'Ah, come on, Milo, gimme a break. Oh, yuck, stinky nappy, and *Friends* is on in a minute.' Having plonked Milo on his changing mat and wrestled with the Pampers, Trudy carries him downstairs. 'Poor little bugger can't sleep, Kev. Now don't you let him fall off the sofa.' Meanwhile, Nick Latimer has just remembered that he left a rather racy art film in the video, and imagines Trudy and Kevin consequently having heavy sex on the sofa. 'Charlotte, we have to go. Sorry, everyone – new babysitter, oik boyfriend, Milo teething . . . you know how it is.'

The Private View

IT'S ALL SO very different from Frimley Green, whence it has taken Gordon and Virginia three hours to reach Whitechapel for the opening of Zoe's first art exhibition. Virginia was so brave about asking the way from hooded men in trainers. 'I say, could you be awfully kind and tell us where we might find the Rampant Cube gallery?' Gordon paled slightly when confronted by burning tyres in a desolate wasteland, but then Zoe emerged from the smoke saying, 'Mum, Dad, what do you think of my installation?' She led Virginia by the hand past what initially appeared to be a very nice privet hedge, labelled *Emasculation*. On closer inspection Virginia discovered it to be topiarised green male genitalia. Gordon, whose social womb is the golf club, is confronted by fierce, stubbly men with facial furniture. 'Well, dear,' he says heartily, 'I feel we're quite in the swim, don't you?' Virginia, whose social mountaineering is normally so tenacious that she's known as Virginia Creeper, is flummoxed by shocking-pink pictures of labia. Where, under the beamed thatch of Honeysuckle Cottage, among the Capo di Monte figurines, did Zoe find inspiration for her oeuvre? How very, very fortunate that they didn't bring Brian and Monica, their best friends from the club, whose son has just qualified as an accountant. It was bad enough Zoe being at art school, but now Monica would be pursing her lips and doing I-Told-You-So.

Virginia, spine stiffened with maternal resolve, faces a tufted carpet sample titled *Pubic Hair* and says briskly to a bald dude in a black T-shirt, 'My daughter did that, you know.' The dude replies in immaculate Etonian, 'Hey, are you Zoe's mother? How incredibly cool.' Gordon bonds with a girl with ginger dreadlocks. 'Splendid, splendid. You shared a flat with Zoe? I bet she never picked washing up off the floor. What it is to be young, eh?' Pioneering back to Surrey, they agree that it was all very interesting.

*Virginia discovered a nice privet hedge, labelled Emasculation,
to be topiarised green male genitalia*

The Hands-On Father

MILO HAS TAKEN Inigo to baby yoga and his art appreciation class on spatial shape awareness, changed his nappy and is now having a macchiato and organic bean salad in Café Tom. Milo is going to meet Cosmo, who's also writing a novel, and they'll talk about urban dislocation while Inigo chews the edge of his animal rag book. 'Hey man, I keep telling Sasha we've got to move to the country. I mean, this is Notting Hill and yet I feel so pressurised, and what is the pollution doing to Inigo? It has to be more intense, I mean, like rising off the pavement, at pushchair level. It could create asthma in his future.' Inigo does Inigo-speak, a chattering cacophony resembling Minoan Greek, to which his father says, 'Yes, little man, of course' and hands him a red felt-tip pen, with which Inigo proceeds to draw on the paternal jeans. 'I shall have these framed for Inigo's first art exhibition. Cosmo, you have to have a child. Until you do, you cannot get in touch with your creative soul. Hey, what about an organic passionfruit ice-cream? Inigo and I will share a couple of spoonfuls. I want to get him used to exotic tastes.' When Inigo was a baby, Milo took him to post-natal classes, massaging his stomach to help alleviate the belly button's sense of loss. When Inigo cried in the night Milo walked round the flat with him, a little square of muslin on his shoulder to catch the dribble. As a banker, Sasha really couldn't be disturbed; she had to fly to Frankfurt at 6am. She was between New York and Tokyo for his first birthday party – 'Milo, he's one, how will he notice? I've had the party bags done by Semmalina, including a cuddly duck. And Philomena will do fabulous egg sandwiches, or whatever babies eat.' And thus she whooshed out of the door in Armani going, 'Bye bye darlings', and Milo whispered, 'It's you and me, little man, against the mad, mad feminine world.'

When Inigo was a baby, Milo took him to post-natal classes,
massaging his stomach to help alleviate the belly button's sense of loss

The Atkins Dieter

JONQUIL IS ADAMANT. No bread – she is not allowed carbo-hydrates on the Atkins Diet – and no wine; the sugar will upset the entire process of her body subsuming its own fat. She will have the fillet steak, medium rare, with sauce béarnaise but no chips. 'The béarnaise is freshly made, isn't it? With organic eggs? I cannot tolerate the preservatives in commercial products.' This four-act play, culminating in the depressing 'Just still water, thank you, sparkling is full of unnecessary sodium,' is incomprehensible to non-Atkins dieters. If Jonquil was having lunch with Jennifer Aniston and Renée Zellweger they could twitter about the joys of protein. But Jonks is lunching with her godfather, who's down from Yorkshire and wants a slap-up meal with a jolly good bottle of burgundy. Not often he gets to take out a pretty young thing; now he's confronted with a zealot burbling about fatty tissue.

For his godson Miles, who has joined them, this is all too horribly familiar. Everyone at his advertising agency is on the Atkins, particularly the men, seduced by the idea of being allowed bacon and egg for breakfast. Now the canteen echoes to the chant of 'Can I eat this?' because nobody can quite be bothered to read Dr Atkins's book. Jonquil – over her green salad with olive oil, no balsamic – is proselytising her regime oblivious to the miasma of boredom descending around the table. The Atkins has changed her life. It's so easy, particularly in restaurants, although going to dinner with friends is a teensy bit tricky. She can't do pasta, or rice, so she just has the vegetables. 'I get on the scales every morning, without clothes, of course, they weigh at least two pounds.' Her godfather is stunned, since Jonquil seems to have come out in her petticoat. The curvaceous teenager who once danced the Duke of Perth with him at the Oban Ball is now the width of a breadstick.

Wine will upset the entire process of Jonquil's body subsuming its own fat

Ben espouses cactus, bamboo and scabrous succulents

The Garden Designer

BEN IS INTO timeless living spaces, the garden as an outdoor room. Style and modernity are his watchwords: there is nothing he cannot achieve with iroko decking, galvanised planters and recessed floor lights. His current diktat on the garden chair is 'oxidised extruded aluminium with polyester mesh'. Speaking in riddles of designer cool is how he subdues clients who express their own opinions – 'I had thought of roses up a trellis, Fantin-Latour perhaps, and honeysuckle, Ben?' – or raise the vulgar question of cost. He isn't known as 'bill and Ben' for nothing; one does not employ him for the geranium-in-terracotta-pot effect. Thus Verity has meekly succumbed to cactus, bamboo and scabrous succulents. Her lawn has been surgically removed and replaced with pebbles. 'Or are we talking Astroturf here, Verity? Astroturf is the new lawn, you just hoover it.' Verity was at least able to gasp faintly that her husband, not to mention the dog, would not condone Astroturf. 'A little too modern, I'm afraid,' adding apologetically, 'would you like some green tea, Ben?' Ben's counter-attack is badinage about copper uplighters, low-voltage stainless-steel downlighters and canvas sails shading Verity's seating area. It would be a shame not to. After all this. And it probably would be best, in the long run, to have the limestone table and the teak ottoman. Ben did Zenka von Spitz's garden in concrete panels washed with ochre and everyone said it was horticulture as theatre, despite the absence of plant life. On the whole, Ben despises plants. Why risk nature when there are Moroccan lanterns, slate tables, Burmese urns and water features? His design at the Chelsea Flower Show contains only a crystal globe spilling water on to sand sparkling with semi-precious stones shipped from Namibia.

The Opera-Goers

LILIAN HAS TRAVELLED by tube from her little flat in Bayswater to Covent Garden. Her splendid paste jewellery – for the opera to her is an occasion, despite the number of vile people wearing jeans – was cunningly concealed under an old Mainbocher coat. Really, these evenings with Geoffrey are a joy. They are just good friends, widow and widower, and Geoffrey gets the No. 11 bus from Sloane Square 'to the Savoy, please, conductor' and then walks up Bow Street. He's always in good time so that he can buy the programmes and get a little champagne organised. Lilian likes a little champagne, a celebratory harbinger of the evening to come. Fizzy, like Mozart, or an essential mainstay if they're doing their annual Wagner. 'I've ordered a bottle, my dear, because I seem to remember that old Tristan takes an entire act to die.' Lilian is so giggly she can't distinguish her Isolde Motif from the Motif of Anguish. Or was it the Motif of Love's Peace or Love's Glance? She consulted Kobbe that afternoon, while having her rest in the flat on the pretty white sofa. Boning up is her contribution to the evening, so she can tell Geoffrey the plot, quite the least she can do when he's been such a love organising supper on the balcony of the Floral Hall in the interval. And Lilian's synopsis saves them having to scrabble for their glasses, peering at the programme at arm's length over the poached salmon.

They both secretly treasure the dear, familiar operas one doesn't have to think about – *Traviata*, *Tosca*, and is there anything more restful than a *Bohème*? – then they can talk about the grandchildren, and whether Geoffrey really should brave a Swan Hellenic cruise to Turkey. When the curtain falls, Geoffrey insists that Lilian has a taxi home, and slips the driver a tenner. Then he gets his No. 11: 'Peter Jones, please, conductor.'

*The opera to them is an occasion, despite the vile people
wearing jeans*

Daddy says does Emerald really want to have done everything by the time she's 15?

The Celebrity Child

EMERALD IS OFF to Ibiza to stay with Jade — the grown-up celebrity child — then she'll join her parents in St Tropez, and they'll all have lunch with Joan at Club 55 before getting on Valentino's yacht. One can't drive anywhere on the Côte d'Azur in summer. Emerald doesn't do traffic. If in doubt, Emerald telephones for Daddy's helicopter. Or Daddy's plane. Toto, the dog, prefers the plane — less noisy — and she has her own travel basket embroidered with 'We're Not In Kansas Any More'. It is part of Emerald's Emerald City range for the Chic Chien, which includes fur bootees for the ski chien in Aspen and matelot lifejackets for the sea chien in Sardinia. Emerald sells on the Shopping Channel and Daddy says her company will float on the stock market soon. Emerald just thinks Toto looks perfectly sweet doing the modelling. Emerald models herself, of course. God, it's sooo boring. She was approached to be the face of Bareface make-up, but she told her agent that, like, it wasn't what she's about. She did a cover for *Tatler* after her business had made its first $10 million, and she'd run away from school in Connecticut with Jomo of Fuzzy Logic, but Daddy said did she really want to have done everything by the time she was 15? The girls at her new school in England thought she was a real loser. Emerald's now going to school in Switzerland where everyone else has real Louis Vuitton bags, too. Right now she wants to have the full chill-out all summer, although Mummy can be really annoying, saying things like, 'Emmy, why are you wearing those heavy boots when it's so hot?' Emerald rolls her eyes and says, 'Because they're cool' and gets on the mobile to P Diddy, with whom she's going clubbing at Les Caves du Roy. Emerald is too young to work out why she has no friends her own age.

Throughout Ascot Week, the chairman's secretary is instructed to inform all callers that Sir Leo is at a meeting, or away on a course

The Powerful Man at Ascot

SIR LEO ROTHWELL has arrived at Ascot by helicopter; he never gives anyone a lift from Westland heliport because the spare seats have to accommodate Lady Rothwell's hat. As they touch down, their chauffeur brings the Bentley alongside and they purr off to Number One car park, in the pleasantly shady space under a tree which Sir Leo's father always had. Sir Leo likes continuity. It is four generations since the Rothwells arrived in London from the Hanseatic ports, bringing their banking skills and the imagination that has resulted in such munificent patronage of the arts and the turf. His black silk topper is inherited from his great-grandfather, who had a horse that should have won the Derby but politely finished second to King Edward VII's. Throughout Ascot Week, the chairman's secretary at Rothwell, Humbert De Groe is instructed to inform all callers that Sir Leo is at a meeting, or away on a course. Both of which are true.

Today the Rothwells are lunching in White's tent, the lobster lunch with extra lobster. The colour matches Lady Rothwell's Chanel suit. They're entertaining Johnny Wetherby, Mark Davies and a light scattering of Keswicks, a splendid preamble to watching Sir Leo's runner in the big race, about which the chauffeur has been given very precise instructions on betting. Tomorrow they will lunch with Stoker Devonshire and the Ascot Authority, Lady Rothwell resplendent in natural pearls from SJ Phillips, her wedding present. As the second, and severely blonde, Lady Rothwell, she has taken her role as the racing wife even unto having her shoes hand-made with low heels for walking to the winner's enclosure. Only dizzy blonde second wives wear stilettos to the Royal Enclosure. On Friday Sir Leo's helicopter will go to Windsor because they are in the royal procession.

The Singleton

LUCINDA'S FRIENDS SAY it is such a pity that she isn't married, she really ought to be since she's so attractive and clever and has such a brilliant career. What they actually mean is why can't they be like her, free to go to the Bliss spa on a Saturday morning? As they are donning layers of hideous quilted clothing in order to watch little Rosie play lacrosse in a blinding east wind, Lucinda is having a leisurely breakfast at the Wolseley: fresh orange juice, eggs Benedict and the newspapers. She's a coiled spring of retail rapacity, ready to unleash her credit card on Bond Street. There'll be lowlights at Michaeljohn, then lunch at Ziani's with her goddaughter, who returns home saying Lucinda's so cool. 'Lucinda's got an Anya bag, Mummy. Lucinda's going to Cape Town for Christmas. Lucinda says I should start having facials.' Mummy's gratitude for this benign interest in her offspring is obliterated by fury that only someone lucky enough to live entirely for themselves could suggest such folderol, and be going to Cape Town, and be thin. Lucinda's married friends haven't time to be thin, since pasta is the quickest thing to cook. Lucinda's fridge contains two bottles of champagne, six bottles of Pellegrino and four little vials of Actimel live organic yogurt. Why would she need anything else when she always eats out?

Her flat is pristine B&B Italia, tables of graphite and lensed glass, chairs like soft suede shells floating on steel frames. All her towels and linen are perfectly white. The married friends, once so tee-hee about having made it up the aisle before Lucinda, now enviously imagine her in cashmere pyjamas in the deep, deep comfort of her solitary bed, while they're sleepless next to a snoring solicitor with hair growing out of his ears.

Lucinda's a coiled spring of retail rapacity

Ho-Phang is deeply worried that Sir and Madam
are so undemanding

The Hotel Butler

GINNY KNOWS THAT these days it is mandatory for every five-star hotel to have a personal butler shimmering in every suite, but she doesn't know what to do with him. In attempts to anticipate her heart's desires, Ho-Phang materialises just as she's about to shave her legs. 'Madam would like water now? Madam's favourite Evian, very cold.' Madam is as grateful as she possibly can be with her back to the wall, clutching a bathmat in front of her. 'Terribly kind, Ho-Phang, how sweet of you. Out on the terrace, perhaps,' and retreats into the bathroom. Bent double, she now peers through the keyhole to see her husband's languid arm reaching out from the sunlounger for his Martini, then Ho-Phang's peerlessly pressed uniform exiting stage left. Swathed in as many clothes as she can get on in 80-degree heat, in case Ho-Phang pops up from behind the DVD/TV fully integrated entertainment centre, she tiptoes on to the terrace, whispering, 'Robert? Has he gone?' Robert, deep in *Stalin: The Court of the Red Tsar* (and rather smug about it), asks has who gone where. 'The butler, Ho-Phang,' she hisses. 'Ah, yes, splendid chap, makes an excellent Martini. He's coming back to draw your bath and sprinkle it with lotus blossoms.'

By day three, a sense of heightened tension is vibrating through the Crusoe Suite. Ho-Phang is deeply worried that Sir and Madam are so undemanding – would they not like champagne or a private barbecue on the beach with flambeaux? Ginny is terrified to put on her bikini in case he sees her cellulite. They spend dinner making a list of pointless tasks to ask him to perform tomorrow, and return to their room to find he has strewn their sheets with hibiscus, making it quite impossible to get into bed. The last three days of their holiday are spent agonising about what to give Ho-Phang as a tip.

*Prue has WC kits bought from the 'Tame the Toilets of the World'
section of a mail-order catalogue*

The Charity Trekker

PRUDENCE IS OF ghostly appearance, smothered in sun screen. The air is thinner at altitude and sunburn is so amateur. Prue is very conscious that she only began climbing a year ago (the Peak District) and now here she is, trekking into the Everest base camp from Lukla. It's for charity, of course. All Prue's family have sponsored her valiant effort on behalf of Save the Crocus. A flyer went out with the parish magazine explaining how the rare wild crocuses in Spring Wood were endangered and now here she is, in the land of the rhododendron, stumping through Nepal to benefit botany. It is really most invigorating. Much of her equipment, bought at vast expense, is a mystery, but she broke in the boots by wearing them to do the shopping at Tesco's.

Having read an article about hydration, she bought a water pipe that runs from her rucksack over her shoulder for constant sipping. 'Got gin and tonic in that, Prue?' ask her fellow trekkers, and she wishes she had, to steady her nerves about the perpetual loo nightmare. Prue is a very private person and scrabbling behind Himalayan boulders with rationed Andrex holds hideous fears for her. She has extraordinary amounts of Imodium, along with WC kits bought from the 'Tame the Toilets of the World' section of an American mail-order catalogue. She forgot her sleeping pills, but is so exhausted by the walking that she clunks out listening to the World Service on the short-wave radio her son bought her. 'Good old Mum, time you had a gap year, off you go and enjoy yourself.' And she is. Prue has chummed up with a yoga teacher and a retired doctor. By the end of the trek, every fingernail will be broken, she'll have ceased to look in the mirror and not washed for a week. But her thighs will be terrifically firm.

The Cosmetic Couple

IT WAS A slippery slope. Alana started with kinesiology, colonic hydrotherapy and radionics, but really Botox is so much easier. As she swore she was never, ever going to be 40, the little trips to Dr Sebagh then became imperative. Particularly after she married Rodolfo; that was when she went to Brazil for the facelift, because it would never do to impugn her new husband's image as a babe magnet. Rodolfo is as sleek as a seal, massaging himself with his own money – an electronics fortune. He goes regularly to a thalassotherapy spa at Quiberon in Brittany, to take the ozone and diet on lobster. He first had a little work on his eyes. After all, he wanted to look fresh and vibrant while directing the full impact of his blue contact lenses at sweet young things in Tramp. Now he looks about 12, and his face is a Kabuki mask; both he and Alana wear their hair well forward to cover the scars. Naturally she's had a boob job, and eats so little that she appears brittle. Rodolfo did his nose in LA – he went in for the morning and came home to Bel-Air with a discreet plaster and an enormous pair of sunglasses. The result is nostrils that appear to have mutated into flared, shiny pink apertures that require Dynorod rather than being blown.

Face on, Rodolfo and Alana are rather marvellous, even if they cannot move any of their features. Gone is the casual insouciance of the raised eyebrow. When they walk through a gala evening at the Metropolitan, or the latest fashionably incomprehensible exhibition at the Serpentine, they take tiny steps because the most recent liposuction hurts so much. They treat themselves and each other as if they are very, very fragile. During summer in the Hamptons Alana and Rodolfo always wear enormous straw hats because the sun would be fatal – one beam and they might blotch or scab, or go up in a little puff of smoke, like Dracula at dawn.

Face on, Rodolfo and Alana are rather marvellous,
even if they cannot move any of their features

Judith can remember the excitement of Dr Kildare

The Soap Addict

JUDITH CONSIDERS IT extraordinarily thoughtless if her son Gerald rings after seven in the evening. By then, she and Clover are tucked up on the sofa, the remote and a savage whisky in hand, for *Emmerdale*. Then it's *Coronation Street* before zapping over to *EastEnders*. Then a little eggy something on a tray while she watches *The Bill*, which she recorded the night before while she was out playing bridge with Helen and Dick. The Queen watches *The Bill* – the only evidence of normality Judith has perceived in that dysfunctional family – but does the Queen also watch *ER*? And, if so, is she concerned about Neela, the British Asian newcomer to the cast who has been branded a 'Third World assassin' by a grumpy fat man on reception? Judith and Clover are most indignant that Dr Corday has been sacked for being over forty. Judith can remember the excitement of *Dr Kildare* when Richard Chamberlain became her schoolgirl pin-up, unsurpassed in the memory even by Simon MacCorkindale in *Casualty*. Judith certainly cannot be interrupted during *Casualty*: poor Charlie has had such a dreadful time recently, Judith truly feels for him, what with Baz, and the red tape with which he is being mummified. Does Mr Blair watch? He should – it would tell him precisely what his wretched policies are doing to the NHS, although perhaps the plot of the woman giving birth on ley lines wouldn't have been one of the more punchy episodes, had he happened upon it.

While Gerald is bemused by his mother's dramatic inner life – 'Well, I suppose she's never lonely' – her grandchildren beg to go and stay. 'Gran's got the best telly.' Nothing annoys Gerald more than his mother having BBC4, and is thus the only person he knows who was able to watch *The Alan Clark Diaries*.

The Trophy Toddler

NATASHA WEARS VIOLET like a matching accessory, heaving her from shopping expeditions at Petit Ange to lunch at Carpaccio, where all the Italian waiters pinch Violet's fat little cheeks, to girly drinks in Eaton Terrace. 'We've just been to Mummy's hairdresser for your first grown-up haircut, haven't we, Violet? And Darren said she had the most beautiful hair, and wouldn't it be cute to put a few lowlights in the front? Show Godmother Celestria, Violet.' Celestria feels nauseated at the thought of a one-year-old having a £150 hair-cut. She has just got engaged, which is the point of the drinks, rather than being a Violet admiration session. 'Engaged! Violet can be a flower girl. When's the wedding? You must wait until September, then she'll be able to walk properly.' Violet's social engagements are noted by her nanny in her Hello Kitty diary. 'Violet is a mini-me networker,' cries Natasha joyously, scooping up the baby mirror image for brunch at Le Caprice, nappies in an Anya Hindmarch bag printed with pictures of Violet and herself.

Spooning tiny bits of organic fish into Violet's rosebud mouth, Natasha tells Celestria (who realises bringing her fiancé along to be introduced was pointless) how she's spent £600 in deposits for the best nursery schools, but of course Violet will go to the Ringrose with Tania Bryer's children and that her first Japanese lessons are already booked in 2005. 'Celestria, you and, erm . . . you both have all this to look forward to. Now, you'll be at Violet's birthday party, won't you? It's a Peter Pan theme and Violet is Tinker Bell because we all believe in fairies. Violet did her first drawing the other day, and we've had it framed for above Daddy's desk, haven't we, baby? Tim is besotted, of course, he's just given Violet a jewellery box.' Violet's first words, after 'Mama', 'No' and 'Mine', are 'Ool box'. The first colour she recognises is Tiffany blue.

'Violet is a mini-me networker,' says Natasha joyously

Margaret steals a cutting, exactly the sort of genteel crime
Wickles Frobisher feared

The Garden Open Day

GEOFFREY IS KEEPING cave while Margaret steals a cutting. Just a teeny one, so as one would hardly notice, but this is exactly the sort of thing Wickles Frobisher feared when she agreed to join the Gardens Scheme. Friends in Norfolk told her that their garden was virtually stripped bare, and if that could happen in Norfolk, nowhere is safe. Wickles has had tortured nights. Her foxtail lilies might be dug up, and the schizophragmas and schisandras savaged on the kitchen garden wall. Margaret, Geoffrey and their ilk will have arrived with trowels and shears secreted in capacious handbags. A security screening device, as at Heathrow, should have been installed in the medieval pigeon house.

Even worse than being raped and pillaged by the middle classes is the idea that there might be nothing worth a little genteel crime. Perhaps the Frobisher sea of dieramas in shades of pink through green would be devastated by an untoward crop circle, or old Jack Frobisher's bog-loving plants trampled by herons, or the hostas reduced to lace doilies by slugs. Wickles had been out in her nightie at midnight fending off their slimy predations by spreading broken eggshells. The village is agog. The garden of Coombe Frobe has never been open to the public before, although the landlord's son once led a guerrilla raid through the ha-ha and had a rave in the tunnelled grotto. No one would have known if he hadn't left his spliffs behind. Hence the tunnelled grotto, studded with seashells by mad old Jack in the 1930s, is a subject of morbid fascination on the scale of the Marabar Caves. Geoffrey and Margaret, taking a high moral stance to make themselves feel better, pronounce the grotto a vulgar conceit. Wickles is only relieved that, at the end of the day, her Kiftsgate remains intact. She purloined the cutting from the garden of friends in Devon.

The Woman Living
with the Builders

THAT'S IT. THE pill, the biscuit, the absolute bitter end. The gasman has driven a nail through the water main, transforming the basement into an indoor swimming-pool. It was to have been Fiona's wonderful world of laundry, a poem of white goods throbbing with washing, ironing board permanently up with Filipina attached. Fiona's girlfriends had been almost as excited by the idea of the sheet roller as by her new pewter Aga – which the chippy is now using as a saw bench. Fiona has put up with the Pleistocene layers of the *Daily Mirror* accumulating in her sitting-room, and the builders' dust, equivalent to the fallout from Pompeii, on the shoulders of her Chanel suits. She has endured the permanent sound of the radio at full volume so that it could be heard above the drilling, and the subsequent result that Dave, Barney and Mitch shout at each other above the orchestral cacophony of drill and Eminem. Fiona has even become accustomed to having the interrogative decibels of 'Cappuccino, mate?' ricocheting off her clenched teeth.

But never, ever did she expect the workmen to use her lavatory. After all she's done for them. The finger bandage when Barney and his hammer had a disagreement; assuaging blood pouring from punctured bits of Mitch, a one-man Savlon alert; the Scotch she gave Dave at Christmas. Now Easter is receding into the distant past and her house, which she and William bought because it needed absolutely nothing doing to it, looks like the Battle of the Somme. The skip, which is costing a fortune, seems entirely full of polystyrene Costa Coffee cups and baguette wrappers; the loo reeks of ciggies (although William says she'd hate it even more if they peed in the garden), and Fiona wants to stop playing nurse and *have her home back*. The builders are deeply puzzled by this sad woman's outbreak of hysteria.

*Fiona has endured the permanent sound of the radio at full volume
so it could be heard above the drilling*

Old ladies can be confident of Jarvis's helping hand

The Bus Conductor

JARVIS HAS BEEN on the 22 for 15 years; before that it was the 19, with a brief interlude on the N25 to Ilford, but he prefers the gents' routes. Old ladies, doddering out of Fortnum's with vital supplies of Earl Grey, can be confident of Jarvis's helping hand. He doesn't let the bus whizz off, precipitating nasty falls, until the halt and the lame are safely seated. Jarvis is an expert with Peter Jones bags – 'Here, let me look after those for you, love' – and puts them in his little cubbyhole until dispensing them courteously at Parson's Green. Old Colonel Pettigrew, who gets on at Green Park after his lunch in White's, knows that if Jarvis is on board he can have a nice little nap all the way to Chelsea Manor Gardens, where Jarvis will wake him and gently decant him on to King's Road. He is unfailingly patient with tourists: the Japanese who have their maps upside down and would be much better on the 11 for the National Gallery; the Americans who want to know the times of the Changing of the Guard and whether Tate Modern is worth visiting. His daughter went on a school outing and says it's cool. She's keen on art, is Joanne, which makes him very proud. Usually the family go back to the West Indies to see their relations each year, the grandparents being frail now, but Jarvis thinks perhaps they should go to Paris so Joanne can get to the Louvre. The fact that you can go by train seems reassuring. Mind you, it's the French tourists who are the noisy ones on the bus, always trying to pay in euros. Putting it on they are, Jarvis reckons. He's firm with trouble, no one fails to pay their fare on his watch and youngsters are firmly deterred from leaping off at the lights. Jarvis's regulars all say that if the 22 becomes one of those horrid modern contraptions with snapping doors where you queue to pay the driver, they'll never travel on the bus again.

Daphne is a one-woman Neighbourhood Watch

The Nosy Neighbour

AUGUST IS WHEN Daphne basks in a lonely glow of popularity. The neighbours who have dismissed her as a frightful curtain-twitcher all year are now supplicants at her door. Bearing gifts of After Eights, they knock, clutching their spare keys and smiling brightly, and say, 'Daphne – hello, how are you? – well, we're off to Tuscany tomorrow and wonder if you could be terribly kind and keep an eye on the house?' They then thrust the keys into her bony hands, together with instructions about feeding the cat and watering the garden. Daphne is fascinated to be a one-woman Neighbourhood Watch. Goodness, Mrs Topham's geraniums are leggy; the Witchetts really should know better than to overwater their pansies. She peeked in the fridge at the Carters and found two bottles of Asti Spumanti. Heavens, isn't that the most frightening hole in the Goldmans' lawn? Either aliens have landed or they have rats. Daphne is, of course, straight on to the council.

Then there is the issue of tree-planting. Daphne has campaigned for more trees in Bassett Road. She has planted roses against the existing trees, which the Witchett fox terrier then peed on. Thus Daphne now Has Something Over Them. Norman Witchett is going to be forced to donate a raffle prize to the local Police Ball in Aid of Fighting Community Crime. Daphne, divorced and training as a psychotherapist, is committed to improving the urban environment and noise restrictions after 10pm. The Carters have had a typed letter about the way their teenagers will talk in the street after parties. 'The cigarette butts I found on our street yesterday are unacceptable. Remember, smoking is the slow way to suicide.' In September, everyone will say, 'Gosh, Daphne, well done, you must come to drinks.' And won't ask her.

The Man About Town

NICK HAS COMPLETED the correct rite of passage for debonair credibility, having escorted Claudia Schiffer and Elle Macpherson, and been snapped pushing the pram of Elizabeth Hurley's baby. Charm is his stock in trade, together with perfect manners, punctuality and the new Mini Cooper S in metallic black with a custom-built Bose sound system. 'Isn't it fun? I just thought my Porsche was too showy in these tough times.' Times have not been noticeably tough at the Omega Gallery. Steven Spielberg popped in the other day for some Horst photographs, the market in the late Herb Ritts is booming, and Nick always rings Bill Wyman if he gets a sniff of a special David Bailey. In his dreams he wants to stage an exhibition by Annie Leibowitz. He imagines a marvellously salacious lesbian publicity coup, as when the Omega banned under-18s from an explicit art series of men's penises – even though it was in black and white.

Meanwhile he is whisking Angel, the latest ditsy blonde super-model, into San Lorenzo. Others might think that the owner, Mara, is a frightful peasant in a cardie, but Nick is all kissy-kissy with her. As someone would be who cannot get a table at Le Caprice. 'I adore Italian food, don't you?' he says to the supermodel-du-jour, whose rictus smile is induced by visions of pasta blowing out her stomach. 'Don't you think truffles smell of sex?' he purrs, forking risotto into his pearly, capped teeth, slightly overlarge signet ring glinting. It doesn't have his family crest on it – tricky if you were born in Purley – but his star sign. 'We Leos are roaring to go, darling.' But he is too clean, too steam-bathed, too pampered at Mayfair's Bath & Racquets Club, too well-shod by Richard James – 'You cannot ever return from handmade' – too safe to wear any tie but Hermes's, to be any-body's intimation of rough.

Charm is his stock in trade

Phyllis said a virus was the last thing they needed at their age

The Luddites

BASIL AND PHYLLIS have finally been converted. Their son, Rupert, a Something-in-the-City, had said, 'Come on, Mum and Dad, you've got to communicate.' Phyllis wondered what was wrong with the telephone, except that her daughter-in-law always seemed too busy to speak to her. Basil thought the odd postcard from the Lost Gardens of Heligan would keep the grandchildren amused. But Rupert gave them his old laptop, said e-mail was 'so cool, Dad, you'll love it. Get on line and I bet you can pull up David Austin's roses.' Basil was very nervous about pulling up anything, particularly from a horticultural god. He and Phyllis had to get in a techno-teacher, such a nice woman. She'd advertised in the parish magazine, and was most reassuring about viruses. Phyllis said that a virus was the last thing they needed at their age; only last year Sars had prevented them from going to Singapore.

Yet now they are becoming nervously competent, and talk with pride of 'surfing the keyboard'. Basil has discovered Amazon, and parcels of books arrive which he'd never previously have bought or read. 'Look, dear, ping that button and it's all done.' Phyllis is very nervous about pinging. When she attempted Waitrose online (as dictated by Rupert) the order arrived with one King Edward potato, seven packets of Persil non-biological, an unripe mango and some coleslaw instead of fresh hummus. 'There you are,' said Phyllis accusingly, 'It's not perfect.' But Basil is now on to a website for CDs. 'Nothing to it, old girl, and we've just had an e-note from little Esme.' 'Dear Gr'ma & Gr'Da. I hope UR Well. I had Kake 4 my birthday. Thk u for my doll.' As Phyllis mourns the tactile pleasure of the thank-you letter, Basil is on to Friends Reunited to find old Chalky from the Marlborough cricket team.

Infinite fiddling is required to achieve Cecil's standard of perfection

The Amateur Photographer

CECIL IS A stranger to the digital camera. 'Not enough pixels, dear boy – you still can't beat a trusty Nikon.' Friends and long-suffering relatives are thus made to stand for hours, rictus 'cheese' grins ossifying on their faces, while Cecil twirls his lenses. 'Nearly there, everyone. Muriel dear, you've got lipstick on your teeth. Anyone got a tissue? Can't have Muriel's pearlies anything less than perfect.' Meanwhile, people's limbs are atrophying while Cecil casts himself on one knee to get the perfect angle, and tinkers with his light meter. Binky Gibbons mutters about automatic focus, but Cecil is gloriously impervious. 'Now, now, Binky, patience, patience. God is in the detail. I don't think the other Cecil – Beaton, don't you know – would have been seduced by automatic focus.' Muriel says under her breath that he was seduced by practically everything else.

With a flurry of clicks, and 'lovely, everyone, lovely' and 'all together now, say "sex"', Cecil has accomplished his oeuvre and is off in search of beguiling grandchildren. This usually results in puzzling pictures of empty chairs and vacant tables as the children are long gone by the time Grandpa has changed his filters and adjusted his f-stops. During summer there is much encouragement for him to go right down the garden and photograph the roses, which are immune to the infinite fiddling required to achieve Cecil's standard of perfection. Indeed, he gave a spirited, if interminable, talk to the WI on the technique of nature photography. The whole family was summoned to witness the slides of his safari in South Africa. 'And there's a monkey. And there's a lion, whoops, upside down, sorry chaps.' The tricky bit is that due to Cecil's painstaking modus operandi most of his photographs are of leopards' bottoms departing the scene.

The Control Freak

PATRICIA IS IN agony. She's allowing the children to decorate the Christmas tree because, after all, one has to, it's part of the ritual of a perfect Christmas, but when they've gone to bed she'll re-do it so all the ornaments are symmetrical. Tinsel is forbidden, as are angels made out of loo rolls. Patricia collects little ornamental shoes for her tree from the Metropolitan Museum shop in New York. She is obsessively making lists so that Christmas looks sublimely effortless. The smoked salmon has been ordered from a remote fishery in North Uist; she spoke to the butcher about the organic, hand-reared bronze-medal turkey in July. The goose is coming from a smallholding in Norfolk. Now she is listing the gory details for the shopping assault on M&S and Waitrose, including vacuum-packed chestnuts. Patricia has no intention of ruining her nails by peeling anything, nor does she do stuffing since it gets stuck in one's rings. There is a great deal of Christmas, particularly the dark cavities of birds, that Patricia can approach only with rubber gloves.

She wrapped all the presents in October, setting up a trestle table in the spare room with jumbo rolls of wrapping-paper bought half-price in the January sales and an industrial-strength Sellotape dispenser. Patricia always keeps ribbon. The stockings are embroidered with the children's names, the dog wears a red bow on the day, and when they return from church on Christmas morning, the champagne is in the fridge and Waitrose's entire stock of blinis are piled with sour cream and caviar. The scented candles ooze winter cinnamony smells, and the gardener has been bribed to come in and light the fire. 'Trisha's a marvel,' everyone says. But if any of the family want to go off-piste from her perfect plans, Patricia looks brutally hurt and goes to her bedroom to cry tears of exhaustion.

Patricia is obsessively making lists so that Christmas looks sublimely effortless

Duane's a busy man, no time to find a parking space

The White Van Man

DUANE IS OBLIVIOUS to the KEEP CLEAR sign because he is parked on top of it, reading the *Star* and talking on his mobile until the silly cow in front gets her arse in gear. Stentorian hooting from school-run mothers, desperate to get their children to Kumon maths coaching, means nothing to Duane. At the most, he will unclamp the telephone from his ear and give the finger to a blonde wearing Juicy Couture. She, convinced that all men in white vans are serial killers, then vainly tries to write his number down in eyeliner on an old parking ticket. Tricky, since Duane has swerved out of sight by cutting up a little old lady with a disabled sticker. Can't hang about, Duane's in deliveries. Bernie the builder wants his grey silicone; Norman the foreman is gagging for his quick grout; Dave the carpenter at Screwit needs his masonry drill bits. The mobile hums with these urgent requests: 'Multi-purpose silicone sealant, mate? Right, I'll pick it up on me way.'

Duane's way is inevitably past the betting shop. Dave's client's a trainer, see? Gave the lads the wink yesterday. On the imperative delivery of acrylic resin masonry finish this afternoon, Dave will pop into the pub to catch the race. The new plasma screen at the Jolly Pilchard is the business. Duane puts two wheels of the van on the pavement outside, lights flashing, just in front of some nice Australians who were attempting to enjoy a European alfresco moment by having their beer and baguettes outside. Duane's a busy man, no time to find a parking space. Look at all his work — that's what those dockets are about in his office, mate. To the uninitiated, Duane's dockets might appear to be odd bits of scrap paper — among the shifting sands of old Red Bull cans, tobacco tins and roll-up papers — and his office the dashboard of his car.

The Female Academic

DAME MURIEL IS renowned for her research into the behavioural patterns of large aquatic rodents. After reading archaeology and anthropology at Newnham in the 1960s (Muriel's mother was probably the only mother of the decade who wished her daughter was hanging out on the King's Road rather than in the unnatural groves of academe) and a PhD at London University, she studied muskrats in Alaska. What Muriel doesn't know about the muskrat isn't worth knowing. She is now analysing domineering female primates in Madagascar. Stout, with grey hair razored into her neck, and sensible shoes, Dame Muriel keeps students spellbound. She is superbly anecdotal; seminars pass in a nanosecond due to her thrilling accounts of the intelligence of lemurs.

Drinking a whisky in the JCR and smoking a cheroot, Muriel booms don't-let-the-bastards-grind-you-down advice at her female students. 'I can remember when a classics don from Corpus Christi refused to dine in college if women were present. Silly old fool. Don't ever confess to an interest in gardening or children. People will think you're a wife.' The parties in her garden flat are a melange of the great, the good and the young. 'Michael? Now you tell Cressida how best to cross the Sahara on a camel. Cressida. This is Michael Palin, he does damn fool things for television. Now where's Peter? Just when I want to talk to him about top-up fees.' Muriel's views on New Labour's education proposals are enough to even discomfort Mr Mandelson. 'You tell that lickspittle PM that the imbalance of male and female lectureships is shocking, and if he really wants more students from underprivileged backgrounds showing unconventional promise, he should ask me.' And so he should. The little aquatic rodent.

Muriel booms don't-let-the-bastards-grind-you-down advice at her female students

'A lone, white sepulchral figure on the beach'

The Overprotected Child

LUCAS IS SLATHERED in factor zillion. He is thus a lone white, sepulchral figure on the beach where other children are brown as nuts. Bertie Bunbury is masterminding a mega-fortification harnessing the incoming tide with a moat, but Lucas is not allowed near the sea unless he wears water wings. This makes it impossible for him to move his arms without biffing Bertie in the face. 'Useless Lucas, run along to Mummy!' chorus the wild and free children, unencumbered by dayglo sun protection suits. Lucas's mother has lectured Mrs Bunbury severely on how skin cancer can be triggered by unprotected exposure to the elements in childhood. Hence the handkerchief sewn into Lucas's sola topi to guard his neck, while the dudes wear baseball caps.

Mrs Bunbury – minimally protected by a Boden bikini – feels sufficiently sorry for Lucas to ask him to join her picnic, but this is disallowed by the presence of crisps, Mars bars and Coca-Cola. Lucas is not permitted foods with E numbers. His dietitian in Harley Street, to whom his mother takes him monthly, says they might make him hyper. His picnic, eaten alone with his mother, consists of raw carrot sticks and an organic chicken sandwich in wheat-free bread. Wheat could make Lucas asthmatic. So at Lily Fairfax's gangsta-pasta party he wasn't able to have any pasta, only the tomato salad provided the tomatoes were skinned for him by Nanny, because the skins can roll up into little spears and pierce the small intestine. Nanny took Lucas home before the video of *Bugsy Malone* because it could overexcite him, he should be reading improving novels. Pizza and McDonald's are denied Lucas, which is why he is found gorging on Jaffa Cakes in the Fairfaxes' larder, and his cred with his peer group is compromised by his mother crying, clutching his sugar-suffused little body to her bosom, and calling him Lulu.

The Christian

VENETIA EXUDES BENIGN radiance. 'What divine canapés!' she exclaims at the appearance of the humble sausage. Old school-friends who've entered the blue eyeshadow zone are warmly embraced and told how wonderful they look. Sad men just dumped by their first wives are given dewy eye-contact as weirdly nice Venetia tells them that she feels their pain. 'I'm so sorry, Hugo. And it must be tough, what with little Freddie and Cecily being so young. But Hugo, can I just tell you that all change is good? We are humbled, but we learn.' Hugo, although beguiled by Venetia's fey, willowy appeal, is not at all sure about the humble bit, or learning anything other than how to get into Venetia's knickers. It is at this point that she announces, 'I am a Christian.' It was only in answer to a simple question about what she did, but Venetia does not consider that her job as an editor at Pulchritude Publishing defines her. She works in the romantic literature section, and is working on herself as a born-again virgin since her baptism – by total immersion – at Holy Trinity Brompton. Hugo et al, having recoiled at the C-word, are now transfixed by the idea of Venetia in a holy wet T-shirt situation. 'Darling, what does one wear for such an event? Did you have to have a bikini wax? Is the font heated?' Venetia, flattered by the interest, realises too late that it is entirely venal. Honestly, men. Her fellow Christians are so much more caring and non-threatening.

Until she became a Christian she was unable to carry the baggage of being a convent girl. Merciless teasing about sexual naughtiness left her shattered. Now Venetia has found a quiet confidence in restraint at the eye of the social storm. No sex before marriage, which will preferably be to a fellow Christian who's a Goldman Sachs partner.

Venetia feels everyone's pain

The Aga Man

PETER ANNOUNCES HIMSELF formally. 'It's the Aga man, madam,' he says when Mrs New-Kitchen opens the door of her Battersea townhouse. Joy of joys, this is the great day: the commissioning of the Aga. Finally the gloss black behemoth dominating the knocked-through, stainless-steel kitchen will growl into life. Mrs N-K cherishes a vision of bubbling casseroles and homemade bread. How long before the Aga will be all systems go? 'She'll take six hours to heat up madam, and she'll weep.' Mrs N-K is horrified, stopping dead in the middle of making Peter a cup of tea. Weep? 'Is, er, she sad about being a London Aga rather than a country Aga?' 'No, madam, it's condensation. You must wipe away the tears with a soft cloth. Two sugars, please.' Mrs N-K now has visions of staying up all night blowing the Aga's nose.

Peter is demonstrating the nifty wrist action required to shift the racks in the ovens. 'Otherwise your roast could shoot out on to the floor. Very unfortunate if the dog's about.' Mrs N-K keenly feels the lack of a black labrador to go with Aga-tha. 'Is, er, her temperature difficult to control. My husband is very concerned about the house becoming too hot.' Mrs N-K doesn't care if she's reduced to running round the kitchen in a bikini in January, but Mr N-K has told her to get some goddamn driving instructions. 'Very unhealthy to be too hot, Caroline. Why you had to have the thing in a little London house, I don't know.' Of course, she's not a thing, she's Mrs N-K's lifestyle statement to her girlfriends. Peter is now waving the toaster. 'Here's your tennis racket, madam. Always heat it under the hot lid first, then your toast won't stick.' Successfully introduced to her new family member, Mrs N-K reflects that it's a long time since anyone called her madam.